· ICE CREAM ·

the perfect weekend treat

· ICE CREAM ·

the perfect weekend treat

Susanna Tee

p

This is a Parragon Publishing Book
First published in 2004

Parragon Publishing
Queen Street House
4 Queen Street
Bath BA1 1HE
United Kingdom

Produced by
The Bridgewater Book Company
Lewes, East Sussex BN7 2NZ
United Kingdom

Photographer Calvey Taylor-Haw
Home Economist Ruth Pollock

ISBN 1-40543-704-9
Printed in China

Notes for the reader
- This book uses imperial, metric, or US cup measurements. Follow the same
  units of measurement throughout; do not mix imperial and metric.
- All spoon measurements are level: teaspoons are assumed to be 5 ml, and
  tablespoons are assumed to be 15 ml.
- Unless otherwise stated, eggs are assumed to be medium.
- Recipes using raw eggs should be avoided by infants, the elderly, pregnant
  women, convalescents, and anyone suffering from an illness.

contents

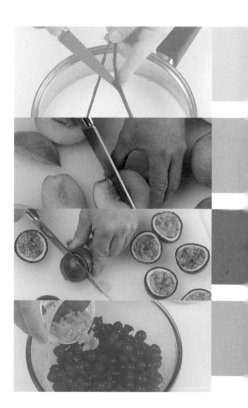

introduction

Few of us can resist licking an ice cream in a cone on a hot summer's day, spooning into a rich, creamy ice cream for dessert or savoring a smooth, cold sherbet after a good meal. Ice cream is probably one of the most popular desserts of all. It is a firm favorite with children and a cool, refreshing choice for adults.

Making your own ice cream or sherbet at home is a surprisingly simple process. If you are lucky enough to own an ice-cream machine, then there is very little effort and time involved. A machine is not essential, however, and you can make successful ice creams without one using the traditional method of beating the ice cream mixture during freezing. The recipes in this book give instructions for making ice creams and sherbets by either method.

Commercial ice cream can be good but nothing can compare to a homemade variety where you know exactly what ingredients have been used. Rich ice creams, sherbets, and frozen desserts can all be found in this collection of recipes. There's no substitute for the real thing, however wicked it may be, so on that note, enjoy!

There's no substitute for the real thing

coolest ic

coolest
ice creams

Who can resist a cool, smooth, indulgent ice cream? The secret of making a smooth ice cream is to beat the mixture in order to break down the ice crystals. An ice-cream machine will do this for you but, made in a freezer, the crystals can easily be beaten halfway through freezing. A food processor efficiently beats the mixture in a matter of moments, although you can also do the beating by hand. The recipes here require you to beat once during freezing but, if you have time, a second beating would not go amiss.

Ice creams taste best if they are not eaten too cold, so take them out of the freezer a short time before serving. Between 15 and 30 minutes is about the right length of time. This also allows the ice cream to soften slightly, which makes it easier to scoop and serve. Alternatively, if you really can't wait, pop the ice cream into the microwave in bursts of 30 seconds until it has softened.

When it comes to serving ice creams, crisp, thin, sweet cookies are the perfect partner for them, so keep a selection of interesting cookies in your pantry to serve at a moment's notice. A stack of cones could be useful too, especially if there are children around. Meringues also make a good accompaniment: a batch of them could easily be whisked up using those left-over egg whites.

The recipes in this chapter are collected from around the world and include a classic Rich Vanilla Ice Cream, an aromatic Indian Kulfi, and a colorful Italian Pistachio Gelato. They are truly cool!

The praline in this recipe has been made with almonds, but blanched hazelnuts, which are the other nuts that praline is traditionally made with, macadamias or pine nuts are equally good.

Chocolate Praline Ice Cream

INGREDIENTS

3 oz/85 g semisweet chocolate, broken into pieces
1¼ cups whole milk
scant ½ cup superfine sugar
3 egg yolks
1¼ cups heavy whipping cream
PRALINE
vegetable oil, for oiling
½ cup granulated sugar
2 tbsp water
scant ⅓ cup blanched almonds

SERVES 4–6

To prepare the praline, brush a baking sheet with oil. Put the sugar, water, and nuts in a large heavy-bottom pan and heat gently, stirring, until the sugar has dissolved, then let the mixture bubble gently for 6–10 minutes, or until lightly golden brown. Do not stir the mixture while it is bubbling and ensure that it does not burn.

As soon as the mixture has turned golden brown, immediately pour it onto the prepared baking sheet and spread it out evenly. Let cool for 1 hour, or until cold and hardened. When the praline has hardened, finely crush it in a food processor or place it in a plastic bag and crush with a hammer.

To prepare the ice cream, put the chocolate and milk in a pan and heat gently, stirring, until the chocolate has melted and the mixture is smooth. Remove from the heat.

Put the sugar and egg yolks in a large bowl and whisk together until pale and the mixture leaves a trail when the whisk is lifted. Slowly add the milk mixture, stirring all the time with a wooden spoon. Strain the mixture into the rinsed-out pan or a double boiler and cook over low heat for 10–15 minutes, stirring all the time, until the mixture thickens enough to coat the back of the spoon. Do not let the mixture boil or it will curdle.

Remove the custard from the heat and let cool for at least 1 hour, stirring from time to time to prevent a skin forming. Meanwhile, whip the cream until it holds its shape. Keep in the refrigerator until ready to use.

If using an ice-cream machine, fold the cold custard into the whipped cream, then churn the mixture in the machine following the manufacturer's instructions. Just before the ice cream freezes, add the praline. Alternatively, freeze the custard in a freezerproof container, uncovered, for 1–2 hours, or until it starts to set around the edges. Turn the custard into a bowl and stir with a fork or beat in a food processor until smooth. Fold in the whipped cream and praline. Return to the freezer and freeze for an additional 2–3 hours, or until firm or required. Cover the container with a lid for storing.

With the addition of chocolate pieces and the chocolate fudge sauce, this is a popular ice cream with children. You could use a generous ½ cup of chocolate chips instead of chopping the chocolate by hand.

Chocolate Chip Ice Cream with Hot Chocolate Fudge Sauce

INGREDIENTS
1¼ cups whole milk
1 vanilla bean
4 oz/115 g milk chocolate
scant ½ cup sugar
3 egg yolks
1¼ cups heavy whipping cream
CHOCOLATE FUDGE SAUCE
1¾ oz/50 g milk chocolate, broken
   into pieces
2 tbsp butter
4 tbsp whole milk
generous 1 cup brown sugar
2 tbsp corn syrup

SERVES 4–6

Pour the milk into a heavy-bottom pan, add the vanilla bean and bring almost to a boil. Remove from the heat and let infuse for 30 minutes. Meanwhile, chop the chocolate into small pieces and set aside.

Put the sugar and egg yolks in a large bowl and whisk together until pale and the mixture leaves a trail when the whisk is lifted. Remove the vanilla bean from the milk, then slowly add the milk to the sugar mixture, stirring all the time with a wooden spoon. Strain the mixture into the rinsed-out pan or a double boiler and cook over low heat for 10–15 minutes, stirring all the time, until the mixture thickens enough to coat the back of the spoon. Do not boil or it will curdle.

Remove the custard from the heat and let cool for at least 1 hour, stirring from time to time to prevent a skin forming. Meanwhile, whip the cream until it holds its shape. Keep in the refrigerator until ready to use.

If using an ice-cream machine, fold the cold custard into the whipped cream, then churn the mixture in the machine following the manufacturer's instructions. Just before the ice cream freezes, add the chocolate pieces. Alternatively, freeze the custard in a freezerproof container, uncovered, for 1–2 hours, or until it starts to set around the edges. Turn the custard into a bowl and stir with a fork or beat in a food processor until smooth. Fold in the whipped cream and chocolate pieces. Return to the freezer and freeze for an additional 2–3 hours, or until firm or required. Cover the container with a lid for storing.

Make the chocolate sauce just before you serve the ice cream. Put the chocolate, butter, and milk in a heatproof bowl set over a pan of simmering water and heat gently, stirring occasionally, until the chocolate has melted and the sauce is smooth. Transfer the mixture to a heavy-bottom pan and stir in the sugar and syrup. Heat gently until the sugar has dissolved, then bring to a boil and boil, without stirring, for 5 minutes. Serve the hot sauce poured over the ice cream.

coolest ice creams 〉 **13**

A traditional English ice cream that was popular at the end of the eighteenth century—the Victorians liked to decorate it with candied violets. There's no reason why you shouldn't do the same.

Brown Bread
Ice Cream

SERVES 4–6

Preheat the oven to 400°F/200°C. Oil a baking sheet, then spread the bread crumbs out on the sheet and sprinkle over the brown sugar. Bake in the oven for 10–15 minutes, stirring occasionally, until the bread crumbs are golden brown and the sugar has caramelized. Let the bread crumbs cool.

When the bread crumbs are cool, using a fork, break up into crumbs again. Pour the heavy and light cream into a large bowl and whip together until the mixture holds its shape. Sift over the confectioners' sugar, then fold into the cream with the vanilla extract and rum, sherry, or Madeira, if using.

If using an ice-cream machine, fold the bread crumbs into the cream mixture, then churn in the machine following the manufacturer's instructions. Alternatively, freeze the cream mixture in a freezerproof container, uncovered, for 1–2 hours, or until it starts to set around the edges. Turn the mixture into a bowl and stir with a fork or beat in a food processor until smooth. Stir in the bread crumbs. Return the ice cream to the freezer and freeze for an additional 2–3 hours, or until firm or required. Cover the container with a lid for storing.

INGREDIENTS

vegetable oil, for oiling

2 cups fresh coarse-textured whole-wheat bread crumbs

generous ¼ cup brown sugar

1¼ cups heavy cream

⅔ cup light cream

½ cup confectioners' sugar

½ tsp vanilla extract

1 tbsp rum, sherry, or Madeira (optional)

This is India's classic ice cream, which is traditionally served at wedding banquets. It derives its rich, characteristic caramel flavor from the milk being cooked for a long time.

Indian Kulfi

INGREDIENTS
6 cups whole milk

12 cardamom pods

scant 1 cup superfine sugar

1 cup shelled pistachios

generous ½ cup ground almonds, plus extra to serve

⅔ cup heavy cream

SERVES 6

Pour the milk into a large heavy-bottom pan and add the cardamom pods. Bring to a boil, then reduce the heat and let simmer for 45 minutes, or until reduced by half. When the milk has reduced, add the sugar, and stir until dissolved. Pour the mixture into a bowl and let cool. When cold, let chill in the refrigerator for at least 8 hours or overnight.

Meanwhile, put the pistachios in a bowl and pour over enough boiling water to cover. Let stand for 1–2 minutes, then drain well. With your fingers, rub off the skins, then slice the pistachios into thin slivers.

When the milk mixture has chilled, strain it through a strainer to remove the cardamom pods. Stir in the ground almonds. Whip the cream until it just holds its shape, then fold into the milk mixture.

If using an ice-cream machine, churn the mixture in the machine following the manufacturer's instructions. Just before the ice cream freezes, add half the slivered pistachios. Alternatively, freeze the mixture in a freezerproof container, uncovered, for 1–2 hours, or until it starts to set around the edges. Turn the mixture into a bowl and stir with a fork or beat in a food processor until smooth. Fold in the whipped cream and half of the slivered pistachios. Return to the freezer and freeze for an additional 2–3 hours, or until firm or required. Cover the container with a lid for storing. Serve with the remaining slivered pistachios sprinkled over the top to decorate.

The short cut of using prepared fresh custard instead of making your own makes this ice cream recipe an easy option. Choose a custard that contains fresh cream or is thick and creamy.

Cinnamon Ice Cream

SERVES 4–6

Pour the cream into a heavy-bottom pan, add the cinnamon and stir together. Bring almost to a boil, then remove from the heat and let infuse for 30 minutes.

Put the custard and lemon juice in a large bowl. Sift in the confectioners' sugar, then stir together. Pour in the cinnamon cream and whisk together until mixed.

If using an ice-cream machine, churn the mixture in the machine following the manufacturer's instructions. Alternatively, freeze the mixture in a freezerproof container, uncovered, for 1–2 hours, or until it starts to set around the edges. Turn the mixture into a bowl and stir with a fork or beat in a food processor until smooth. Return to the freezer and freeze for an additional 2–3 hours, or until firm or required. Cover the container with a lid for storing.

INGREDIENTS
1¼ cups heavy whipping cream
1 tsp ground cinnamon
scant 2½-cup carton fresh custard
1 tbsp lemon juice
scant ½ cup confectioners' sugar

When you have finished with the vanilla bean, don't discard it. Rinse it under cold water, let dry, then place it in a jar of superfine sugar to make your own vanilla sugar.

Rich Vanilla Ice Cream

INGREDIENTS
1¼ cups light cream and
   1¼ cups heavy cream or
   2½ cups heavy whipping cream
1 vanilla bean
4 large egg yolks
generous ½ cup superfine sugar

SERVES 4–6

Pour the light and heavy cream or heavy whipping cream into a large heavy-bottom pan. Split open the vanilla bean and scrape out the seeds into the cream, then add the whole vanilla bean too. Bring almost to a boil, then remove from the heat and let infuse for 30 minutes.

Put the egg yolks and sugar in a large bowl and whisk together until pale and the mixture leaves a trail when the whisk is lifted. Remove the vanilla bean from the cream, then slowly add the cream to the egg mixture, stirring all the time with a wooden spoon. Strain the mixture into the rinsed-out pan or a double boiler and cook over low heat for 10–15 minutes, stirring all the time, until the mixture thickens enough to coat the back of the spoon. Do not let the mixture boil or it will curdle. Remove the custard from the heat and let cool for at least 1 hour, stirring from time to time to prevent a skin forming.

If using an ice-cream machine, churn the cold custard in the machine following the manufacturer's instructions. Alternatively, freeze the custard in a freezerproof container, uncovered, for 1–2 hours, or until it starts to set around the edges. Turn the custard into a bowl and stir with a fork or beat in a food processor until smooth. Return to the freezer and freeze for an additional 2–3 hours, or until firm or required. Cover the container with a lid for storing.

You could use instant coffee granules instead of the freshly ground coffee but the flavor will not be so distinctive.

Cappuccino Ice Cream

SERVES 4

Pour the milk and 2 cups of the cream into a heavy-bottom pan, stir in the coffee, and bring almost to a boil. Remove from the heat, let infuse for 5 minutes, then strain through a paper filter or a strainer lined with cheesecloth.

Put the egg yolks and sugar in a large bowl and whisk together until pale and the mixture leaves a trail when the whisk is lifted. Slowly add the milk mixture, stirring all the time with a wooden spoon. Strain the mixture into the rinsed-out pan or a double boiler and cook over low heat for 10–15 minutes, stirring all the time, until the mixture thickens enough to coat the back of the spoon. Do not let the mixture boil or it will curdle. Remove the custard from the heat and let cool for at least 1 hour, stirring from time to time to prevent a skin forming.

If using an ice-cream machine, churn the cold custard in the machine following the manufacturer's instructions. Alternatively, freeze the custard in a freezerproof container, uncovered, for 1–2 hours, or until it starts to set around the edges. Turn the custard into a bowl and stir with a fork or beat in a food processor until smooth. Return to the freezer and freeze for an additional 2–3 hours, or until firm or required. Cover the container with a lid for storing.

To serve, whip the remaining cream until it holds its shape. Scoop the ice cream into wide-brimmed coffee cups and smooth the tops. Spoon the whipped cream over the top of each and sprinkle with unsweetened cocoa. Decorate with chocolate-coated coffee beans.

INGREDIENTS

⅔ cup whole milk
2½ cups heavy whipping cream
4 tbsp finely ground fresh coffee
3 large egg yolks
generous ½ cup superfine sugar
unsweetened cocoa, for dusting
chocolate-coated coffee beans,
    to decorate

This recipe uses evaporated milk instead of a custard base. Keep a can in the refrigerator so that the evaporated milk is chilled and ready for use. This is important for enabling the milk to be whisked.

Maple Syrup & Walnut Ice Cream

INGREDIENTS
scant 1 cup walnut pieces
⅔ cup maple syrup
1¼ cups heavy cream
7 fl oz/200 ml canned evaporated milk, well chilled

SERVES 6

Put the walnut pieces in a food processor and process until finely chopped but be careful not to process them into a purée. Set aside.

Mix the syrup and cream together until well blended. Pour the chilled evaporated milk into a large bowl and whisk until thick and doubled in volume. The mixture should leave a trail when the whisk is lifted. Add the syrup mixture to the whisked milk and fold together.

If using an ice-cream machine, churn the mixture in the machine following the manufacturer's instructions. Just before the ice cream freezes, add the chopped nuts. Alternatively, freeze the mixture in a freezerproof container, uncovered, for 1–2 hours, or until it starts to set around the edges. Turn the mixture into a bowl and stir with a fork or beat in a food processor until smooth. Stir in the chopped nuts, then return to the freezer and freeze for an additional 2–3 hours, or until firm or required. Cover the container with a lid for storing.

The sauce is extremely easy to make in a microwave. Simply put all the ingredients in a medium bowl or pitcher and cook on High for 3 minutes, stirring several times, until melted.

Ginger Ice Cream with Hot Chocolate Sauce

INGREDIENTS
1¼ cups whole milk
3 egg yolks
scant ½ cup brown sugar
1¼ cups heavy whipping cream
1¾ oz/55 g preserved ginger
1 tbsp preserved ginger syrup
HOT CHOCOLATE SAUCE
6 oz/175 g semisweet chocolate, broken
    into pieces
2 tbsp butter
3 tbsp corn syrup
3 tbsp whole milk

SERVES 4–6
Pour the milk into a heavy-bottom pan and bring almost to a boil. Remove from the heat. Put the egg yolks and sugar in a large bowl and whisk together until pale and the mixture leaves a trail when the whisk is lifted. Slowly add the milk, stirring all the time with a wooden spoon. Strain the mixture into the rinsed-out pan or a double boiler and cook over low heat for 10–15 minutes, stirring all the time, until the mixture thickens enough to coat the back of the spoon. Do not let the mixture boil or it will curdle. Remove the custard from the heat and let cool for at least 1 hour, stirring from time to time to prevent a skin forming.

Meanwhile, whip the cream until it holds its shape. Keep in the refrigerator until ready to use. Finely chop the preserved ginger. When the custard is cold, stir the preserved ginger syrup into it but not the chopped ginger at this stage.

If using an ice-cream machine, fold the cold custard into the whipped cream, then churn the mixture in the machine following the manufacturer's instructions. Just before the ice cream freezes, add the chopped preserved ginger. Alternatively, freeze the custard in a freezerproof container, uncovered, for 1–2 hours, or until it starts to set around the edges. Turn the custard into a bowl and stir with a fork or beat in a food processor until smooth. Fold in the whipped cream and chopped preserved ginger. Return to the freezer and freeze for an additional 2–3 hours, or until firm or required. Cover the container with a lid for storing.

Make the hot chocolate sauce just before you are going to serve the ice cream. Put the ingredients in a heatproof bowl set over a saucepan of simmering water and heat gently, stirring occasionally, until the chocolate has melted and the sauce is smooth. Serve the hot sauce poured over the ice cream.

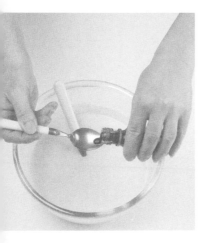

Real Italian ice cream has a soft texture because, as in this recipe, it is made with milk and contains no cream. If you are using the green food coloring, add it very slowly, drop by drop.

Italian Pistachio Gelato

INGREDIENTS
3½ cups whole milk

1 vanilla bean

9 egg yolks

scant 1 cup superfine sugar

2 tbsp almond-flavored liqueur (optional)

few drops of green food coloring
(optional)

1 cup shelled pistachios

SERVES 6–8
Pour the milk into a heavy-bottom pan, add the vanilla bean, and bring almost to a boil. Remove from the heat and let infuse for 15 minutes.

Put the egg yolks and sugar in a large bowl and whisk together until pale and the mixture leaves a trail when the whisk is lifted. Remove the vanilla bean from the milk, then slowly add the milk to the egg mixture, stirring all the time with a wooden spoon. Strain the mixture into the rinsed-out pan or a double boiler and cook over low heat for 10–15 minutes, stirring all the time, until the mixture thickens enough to coat the back of the spoon. Do not let the mixture boil or it will curdle.

Remove the custard from the heat and let cool for at least 1 hour, stirring from time to time to prevent a skin forming. When the custard is cold, stir in the liqueur, if using, and, if wished, add the food coloring to tint the mixture pale green. Finely chop the nuts.

If using an ice-cream machine, churn the cold custard in the machine following the manufacturer's instructions. Just before the ice cream freezes, add the chopped nuts. Alternatively, freeze the custard in a freezerproof container, uncovered, for 1–2 hours, or until it starts to set around the edges. Turn the custard into a bowl and stir with a fork or beat in a food processor until smooth. Stir in the chopped nuts, then return to the freezer and freeze for an additional 2–3 hours, or until firm or required. Cover the container with a lid for storing.

the fruit bowl

Fresh fruit desserts are always popular, and soft berries and citrus fruits all blend beautifully with fresh cream and yogurt to make luscious fruit ice creams. The only rule is that you must choose the freshest, ripest, most unblemished fruits. Make the recipes to be found here when the fruits are in season and plentiful. From Rippled Black Currant Ice Cream to Fresh Peach Ice Cream and Crushed Cherry Ice Cream to Dairy Strawberry Ice Cream, you can provide instant desserts throughout the summer.

Fruit ice creams in particular look stunning and impressive when served in an ice bowl inlaid with fresh fruit and leaves. An ice bowl is surprisingly easy to make: take a 6-cup ovenproof bowl and, if wished, line the base and sides with slices of orange or lemon and mint, lemon balm, or scented geranium leaves.

Insert a 4-cup ovenproof bowl inside and fill the space between the two bowls with water. Immediately place a plate and a heavy weight on top. Put in the freezer for at least 4 hours, until frozen or required. To use the ice bowl, run the bowls under hot water until they loosen, then quickly transfer the ice bowl to a serving plate and return to the freezer until ready to fill.

For an attractive finishing touch, serve the ice creams with more of the fresh fruits from which they were made. A few fresh strawberries, some orange segments, a sprinkling of raspberries, or a whole cherry popped on top makes all the difference.

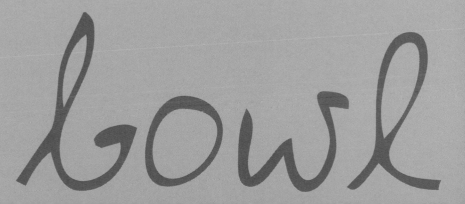

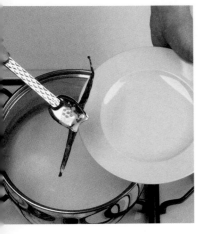

Other varieties of rippled fruit ice cream, such as raspberry and strawberry, can be made in the same way. Simply substitute the black currants with your chosen fruit.

Rippled Black Currant Ice Cream

INGREDIENTS
scant 2 cups whole milk
1 vanilla bean
generous 1¼ cups superfine sugar
4 egg yolks
scant 2 cups fresh black currants,
    plus extra to decorate
6 tbsp water
scant 2 cups heavy whipping cream

SERVES 6–8

Pour the milk into a heavy-bottom pan, add the vanilla bean, and bring almost to a boil. Remove from the heat and let infuse for 30 minutes.
Put scant ⅔ cup of the sugar and the egg yolks in a large bowl and whisk together until pale and the mixture leaves a trail when the whisk is lifted. Remove the vanilla bean from the milk, then slowly add the milk to the sugar mixture, stirring all the time with a wooden spoon. Strain the mixture into the rinsed-out pan or a double boiler and cook over low heat for 10–15 minutes, stirring all the time, until the mixture thickens enough to coat the back of the spoon. Do not let the mixture boil or it will curdle. Remove the custard from the heat and let cool for at least 1 hour, stirring from time to time to prevent a skin forming.

Meanwhile, strip the black currants from their stalks using the tines of a fork and put them in a heavy-bottom pan with the remaining sugar and the water. Heat gently, stirring, until the sugar has dissolved, then let simmer gently for 10 minutes, or until the black currants are very soft.

Push the black currants through a nylon strainer into a bowl to remove the seeds, then let the purée cool. Meanwhile, whip the cream until it holds its shape. Keep in the refrigerator until ready to use.

If using an ice-cream machine, fold the cold custard into the whipped cream, then churn the mixture in the machine following the manufacturer's instructions. Just before the ice cream freezes, spread half in a freezerproof container. Pour

over half the black currant purée, then repeat the layers. Freeze for 1–2 hours, or until firm or required. Alternatively, freeze the custard in a freezerproof container, uncovered, for 1–2 hours, or until it starts to set around the edges. Turn the custard into a bowl and stir with a fork or beat in a food processor until smooth. Fold in the whipped cream. Spread half back into the container, then pour over half the black currant purée. Repeat the layers. Return to the freezer and freeze for 2–3 hours, or until firm or required. Cover the container with a lid for storing. Serve decorated with black currants.

The strained plain yogurt makes this smooth and creamy. For an orange version, use 6 tablespoons of frozen concentrated, unsweetened orange juice instead of the lemon juice.

Lemon Yogurt Ice Cream

INGREDIENTS
2–3 lemons

scant 2½-cup carton strained
    plain yogurt

⅔ cup heavy cream

½ cup superfine sugar

finely pared lemon rind, to decorate

SERVES 4–6
Squeeze the juice from the lemons—you need 6 tablespoons in total. Put the juice into a bowl, add the yogurt, cream, and sugar, and mix well together.

If using an ice-cream machine, churn the mixture in the machine following the manufacturer's instructions. Alternatively, freeze the mixture in a freezerproof container, uncovered, for 1–2 hours, or until it starts to set around the edges. Turn the mixture into a bowl and stir with a fork or beat in a food processor until smooth. Return to the freezer and freeze for an additional 2–3 hours, or until firm or required. Cover the container with a lid for storing. Serve with finely pared lemon rind.

When choosing store-bought ice cream, always buy a variety that is described as "dairy." This contains a proportion of heavy cream, as opposed to others that are made with only vegetable fat.

Dairy Strawberry Ice Cream

SERVES 6

Put the sugar and water in a heavy-bottom pan and heat gently, stirring, until the sugar has dissolved. Bring to a boil, then, without stirring, boil for 5 minutes to form a syrup. Toward the end of the cooking time, keep an eye on the mixture to ensure that it does not burn. Immediately remove the syrup from the heat and let cool for at least 1 hour.

Meanwhile, push the strawberries through a nylon strainer into a bowl to form a purée. When the syrup is cold, add the strawberry purée to it with the lemon juice and orange juice and stir well together. Whip the cream until it holds its shape. Keep in the refrigerator until ready to use.

If using an ice-cream machine, fold the strawberry mixture into the whipped cream, then churn in the machine following the manufacturer's instructions. Alternatively, freeze the mixture in a freezerproof container, uncovered, for 1–2 hours, or until it starts to set around the edges. Turn the mixture into a bowl and stir with a fork or beat in a food processor until smooth. Fold in the whipped cream. Return to the freezer and freeze for an additional 2–3 hours, or until firm or required. Cover the container with a lid for storing. Serve decorated with strawberries.

INGREDIENTS
generous 1 cup superfine sugar
⅔ cup water
2 lb/900 g fresh strawberries, plus extra to decorate
juice of ½ lemon
juice of ½ orange
1¼ cups heavy whipping cream

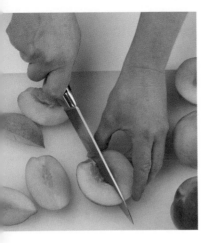

A delightful ice cream to serve in summer, this recipe uses sweetened condensed milk instead of custard, which makes it very simple and quick to prepare.

Fresh Peach Ice Cream

INGREDIENTS

4 ripe peaches

1¼ cups canned sweetened
    condensed milk

juice of 1 lemon

1¼ cups heavy whipping cream

toasted slivered almonds, to decorate

SERVES 6

Cut the peaches into quarters with a sharp knife, remove the pits, then peel off the skins. Coarsely chop the peach flesh.

Put the chopped peaches, sweetened condensed milk, and lemon juice in a food processor or blender and process to form a purée. Push the mixture through a nylon strainer into a bowl to remove the brown flecks of flesh. Whip the cream until it holds its shape. Keep in the refrigerator until ready to use.

If using an ice-cream machine, fold the whipped cream into the peach mixture, then churn in the machine following the manufacturer's instructions. Alternatively, freeze the mixture in a freezerproof container, uncovered, for 1–2 hours, or until it starts to set around the edges. Turn the mixture into a bowl and stir with a fork or beat in a food processor until smooth. Fold in the whipped cream. Return to the freezer and freeze for an additional 2–3 hours, or until firm or required. Cover the container with a lid for storing. Serve decorated with toasted slivered almonds.

To serve this ice cream in the empty orange halves, cut around the inside of the oranges with a serrated knife and scoop out the flesh. Keep the orange shells in the freezer until you are ready.

Orange Ice Cream

SERVES 6–8

Pour the milk into a pan and bring almost to a boil. Remove from the heat. Put the sugar and egg yolks in a large bowl and whisk together until pale and the mixture leaves a trail when the whisk is lifted. Slowly add the milk, stirring all the time with a wooden spoon. Strain the mixture into the rinsed-out pan or a double boiler and cook over low heat for 10–15 minutes, stirring all the time, until the mixture thickens enough to coat the back of the spoon. Do not let the mixture boil or it will curdle. Remove the custard from the heat and let cool for at least 1 hour, stirring from time to time to prevent a skin forming.

Meanwhile, finely grate the rind from 1 of the oranges and squeeze the juice from all 3 oranges—you should have about 1½ cups of juice in total. If wished, set aside the orange skins for serving (see above). Whip the cream until it just holds its shape. Keep in the refrigerator until ready to use. When the custard is cold, add the orange rind and juice and mix well together.

If using an ice-cream machine, fold the cold custard into the whipped cream, then churn the mixture in the machine following the manufacturer's instructions. Alternatively, freeze the custard in a freezerproof container, uncovered, for 1–2 hours, or until it starts to set around the edges. Turn the custard into a bowl and stir with a fork or beat in a food processor until smooth. Fold in the whipped cream. Return to the freezer and freeze for an additional 2–3 hours, or until firm or required. Cover the container with a lid for storing. Serve with the orange segments.

INGREDIENTS
1¼ cups whole milk
scant ½ cup superfine sugar
3 egg yolks
1¼ cups heavy cream
3 large oranges, plus 3 extra oranges, segmented, to serve

It is the Italian mascarpone cheese that gives this ice cream its creaminess, but any other rich, fresh cheese can be used. Bottled lime juice, instead of fresh, makes it simple to prepare.

Lime & Mascarpone Ice Cream

INGREDIENTS
½ cup bottled lime juice
    or cordial
1 lb 2 oz/500 g mascarpone cheese
1½ cups confectioners' sugar
⅔ cup heavy whipping cream

SERVES 4–6
Put the lime juice in a bowl, add the mascarpone, and beat together. Sift the confectioners' sugar into the mixture and beat again until well blended. Whip the cream until it holds its shape. Keep in the refrigerator until ready to use.

If using an ice-cream machine, fold the whipped cream into the mascarpone mixture, then churn in the machine following the manufacturer's instructions. Alternatively, freeze the mixture in a freezerproof container, uncovered, for 1–2 hours, or until it starts to set around the edges. Turn the mixture into a bowl and stir with a fork or beat in a food processor until smooth. Fold in the whipped cream. Return to the freezer and freeze for an additional 2–3 hours, or until firm or required. Cover the container with a lid for storing.

This is a very rich ice cream. Omit the rum if serving it to children. You can make Avocado Ice Cream following the same recipe. Simply replace the bananas with 2 large avocados.

Banana Ice Cream

SERVES 8

Peel and slice the bananas, then put the flesh in a food processor or blender. Add the lemon juice and process to form a very smooth purée. Turn the mixture into a large bowl. Alternatively, sprinkle the lemon juice over the banana slices, then push the flesh through a nylon strainer to form a purée. Add the rum, if using, and mix well together.

Sift the confectioners' sugar into the mixture and beat until well mixed. Whip the cream until it holds its shape. Keep in the refrigerator until ready to use.

If using an ice-cream machine, fold the whipped cream into the banana mixture, then churn the mixture in the machine following the manufacturer's instructions. Alternatively, freeze the mixture in a freezerproof container, uncovered, for 1–2 hours, or until it starts to set around the edges. Turn the mixture into a bowl and stir with a fork or beat in a food processor until smooth. Fold in the whipped cream. Return to the freezer and freeze for an additional 2–3 hours, or until firm or required. Cover the container with a lid for storing.

INGREDIENTS
3 bananas
2 tbsp lemon juice
1 tbsp white rum (optional)
1 cup confectioners' sugar
2½ cups heavy whipping cream

If you have a fresh coconut, its grated flesh can be used instead of the dry unsweetened coconut. Malibu is a coconut-flavored liqueur, which blends well with the ice cream, but you could use white rum.

Coconut Ice Cream with Tropical Fruits

INGREDIENTS

2½ cups coconut milk
scant 1 cup superfine sugar
6 egg yolks
1⅓ cups dry unsweetened coconut
⅔ cup heavy cream
1 tbsp Malibu (optional)

TROPICAL FRUITS

2 papayas, peeled and seeded
2 carambola
2 kiwifruit, peeled
1 tbsp superfine sugar
4 tbsp Malibu (optional)

SERVES 6

Pour the coconut milk into a pan and heat gently. Remove from the heat. Put the sugar and egg yolks in a large bowl and whisk together until pale and the mixture leaves a trail when the whisk is lifted. Slowly add the coconut milk, stirring all the time with a wooden spoon. Strain the mixture into the rinsed-out pan or a double boiler and cook over low heat for 10–15 minutes, stirring all the time, until the mixture thickens enough to coat the back of the spoon. You may find that the mixture starts to separate, and if it does, simply whisk it vigorously until it is smooth again. Do not let the mixture boil or it will curdle.

Remove the custard from the heat, stir in the dry unsweetened coconut, then let cool for at least 1 hour, stirring from time to time to prevent a skin forming.

Meanwhile, whip the cream until it just holds its shape. Keep in the refrigerator until ready to use. When the custard is cold, add the Malibu, if using, and mix well together.

If using an ice-cream machine, fold the cold custard into the whipped cream, then churn the mixture in the machine following the manufacturer's instructions. Alternatively, freeze the custard in a freezerproof container, uncovered, for 1–2 hours, or until it starts to set around the edges. Turn the custard into a bowl and stir with a fork or beat in a food processor until smooth. Fold in the whipped cream. Return to the freezer and freeze for an additional 2–3 hours, or until firm or required. Cover the container with a lid for storing.

To prepare the tropical fruits, thinly slice and put in a large shallow dish. Sprinkle the sugar and Malibu, if using, over the fruit, then cover and let chill in the refrigerator for 2–3 hours before serving with the ice cream.

To make a raspberry or strawberry version, replace the cherries with the appropriate fresh fruit. For a peach or apricot version, use 15 oz/425 g canned fruit in syrup and ⅔ cup of the syrup.

Crushed Cherry Ice Cream

SERVES 6

Put the sugar and water in a heavy-bottom pan and heat gently, stirring, until the sugar has dissolved, then bring to a boil and boil for 3 minutes. Reduce the heat, add the cherries, and let simmer gently for about 10 minutes, or until soft. Let the mixture cool for at least 1 hour.

When the cherries are cold, put them in a food processor or blender with the syrup. Add the orange juice and process the cherries until just coarsely chopped. Do not blend too much as the cherries should just be crushed, not puréed. Pour the heavy and light cream into a large bowl and whip together until the mixture holds its shape. Fold in the crushed cherries.

If using an ice-cream machine, churn the mixture in the machine following the manufacturer's instructions. Alternatively, freeze the mixture in a freezerproof container, uncovered, for 1–2 hours, or until it starts to set around the edges. Turn the mixture into a bowl and stir with a fork or beat in a food processor until smooth. Return to the freezer and freeze for an additional 2–3 hours, or until firm or required. Cover the container with a lid for storing. Serve decorated with whole cherries.

INGREDIENTS
½ cup sugar
⅔ cup water
1¼ cups fresh cherries, pitted, plus extra whole cherries to decorate
2 tbsp freshly squeezed orange juice
1¼ cups heavy cream
⅔ cup light cream

Cream Crowdie is often considered the national dessert of Scotland. It consists of oatmeal, heavy cream, and Drambuie with optional raspberries. Here the dessert has been turned into an ice cream.

Cream Crowdie Ice Cream

INGREDIENTS

2¾ oz/75 g coarse oatmeal

2½ cups heavy whipping cream

½ cup superfine sugar

2 tbsp Drambuie

2 tbsp honey (preferably heather)

scant 1 cup fresh raspberries,
    plus extra to decorate

SERVES 6

Preheat the oven to 350°F/180°C. Spread the oatmeal out on a baking sheet and bake in the oven for about 10 minutes, tossing the oatmeal several times during the cooking time so that it browns evenly. Remove from the oven and let cool for 30 minutes.

Pour the cream into a large bowl, add the sugar, and whip until the cream holds its shape. Add the Drambuie and honey and fold in until well blended.

If using an ice-cream machine, churn the mixture in the machine following the manufacturer's instructions. Just before the ice cream freezes, add the toasted oatmeal and raspberries. Alternatively, freeze the mixture in a freezerproof container, uncovered, for 1–2 hours, or until it starts to set around the edges. Turn the mixture into a bowl and stir with a fork or beat in a food processor until smooth. Fold in the toasted oatmeal and the raspberries, then return to the freezer and freeze for an additional 2–3 hours, or until firm or required. Cover the container with a lid for storing. Serve sprinkled with raspberries.

all iced up

Clean-tasting sherbets, or water ices, make a refreshing dessert to finish a rich meal, but they can also be served between courses to cleanse the palate. Savory sherbets, such as the Fresh Mint Sherbet, can be served as an appetizer. Sherbets are made from a sugar syrup, flavored with fruit juice, fruit purée, wine, liqueur, tea, or herbs and sometimes contain egg whites to make them lighter. A wide variety of sherbets can be found in this chapter, for example Coffee Granita, an Italian water ice that is served broken into small ice crystals, and Gooseberry and Elderberry Flower Sherbet, which is slightly creamy but not as creamy as an ice cream.

Like ice creams, sherbets made in the freezer need to be beaten during the freezing process to produce a smooth texture. If you own an ice-cream machine, then this is done for you. If you don't and you would rather not have to return to the freezer to beat the mixture, then try the recipe for Raspberry Parfait where the beating is done at the preparation stage.

Made in a machine, sherbets can be served freshly churned, but if frozen in the freezer, they need to be left to soften for about 10 minutes at room temperature prior to serving. Sherbets look their most elegant when served in individual glasses. If convenient, they can be scooped out well ahead of time and stored in the freezer on trays lined with nonstick parchment paper. The scoops can then be piled into chilled glasses and served.

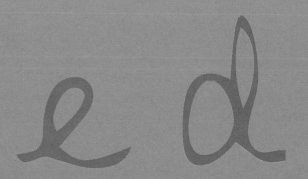

A particularly refreshing sherbet, it is ideal served as an appetizer or a palate-cleanser between courses. If wished, extra chopped fresh mint can be stirred in just before it freezes firmly.

Fresh Mint Sherbet

SERVES 4–6

Put the sugar and water in a heavy-bottom pan and heat gently, stirring, until the sugar has dissolved. Bring to a boil, then cook, without stirring, over medium heat for 2 minutes. Remove from the heat and let cool slightly.

Meanwhile, strip the mint leaves from their stems and put the leaves in a food processor. Pour the syrup over the mint leaves, then process until they are very finely chopped. Let cool, then chill the mint syrup in the refrigerator for 2 hours, or until cold.

Squeeze the juice from the lemons and measure out ½ cup. Add the juice to the mint syrup, then strain the mixture through a nylon strainer.

If using an ice-cream machine, churn the mixture in the machine following the manufacturer's instructions. Alternatively, freeze the mixture in a freezerproof container, uncovered, for 3–4 hours, or until mushy. Turn the mixture into a bowl and stir with a fork or beat in a food processor to break down the ice crystals. Return the sherbet to the freezer and freeze for an additional 3–4 hours, or until firm or required. Cover the container with a lid for storing. Serve decorated with mint sprigs.

INGREDIENTS
generous 1 cup sugar

1¼ cups water

2¼ oz/60 g fresh mint, plus extra sprigs to decorate

3–4 lemons

Choose mangoes that are juicy and ripe to make this sherbet. To test for ripeness, smell them. A ripe mango gives off a noticeable fragrance.

Mango Sherbet

INGREDIENTS
2 large ripe mangoes
juice of 1 lemon
pinch of salt
generous ½ cup sugar
3 tbsp water

SERVES 4–6

Using a sharp knife, thinly peel the mangoes, holding them over a bowl to catch the juices. Cut the flesh away from the central seed and put in a food processor or blender. Add the mango juice, lemon juice, and salt and process to form a smooth purée. Push the mango purée through a nylon strainer into the bowl.

Put the sugar and water in a heavy-bottom pan and heat gently, stirring, until the sugar has dissolved. Bring to a boil, without stirring, then remove from the heat and let cool slightly.

Pour the syrup into the mango purée and mix well together. Let cool, then chill the mango syrup in the refrigerator for 2 hours, or until cold.

If using an ice-cream machine, churn the mixture in the machine following the manufacturer's instructions. Alternatively, freeze the mixture in a freezerproof container, uncovered, for 3–4 hours, or until mushy. Turn the mixture into a bowl and stir with a fork or beat in a food processor to break down the ice crystals. Return to the freezer and freeze for an additional 3–4 hours, or until firm or required. Cover the container with a lid for storing.

Granita is an Italian sherbet or water ice, which is broken into small ice crystals and served in tall glasses. It is cooling on a hot day and is a suitable dessert after a substantial dinner.

Coffee Granita

SERVES 6

Put the sugar and water in a heavy-bottom pan and heat gently, stirring, until the sugar has dissolved. Bring to a boil, then remove from the heat and stir in the coffee. Let infuse for 1 hour and become cold.

Strain the coffee through a paper filter or a strainer lined with cheesecloth. Pour the coffee into 2 shallow freezerproof containers and freeze, uncovered, for 30 minutes.

Turn both mixtures into a bowl and stir with a fork, or beat in a food processor, to break down the ice crystals. Return to the freezer and freeze, repeating the breaking down of the ice crystals about every 30 minutes until the granita is granular. This process will take 3–4 hours in total. Cover the container with a lid for storing.

Serve the granita in glasses, straight from the freezer, broken into tiny ice crystals. Top each glass with a little whipped cream.

INGREDIENTS
2 tbsp sugar
2½ cups water
1¾ oz/50 g fresh Italian coffee, finely ground
½ cup heavy whipping cream, whipped, to serve

It is possible to use a variety of soft fruits in this recipe, although you won't necessarily end up with a red berry sorbet! Choose from strawberries, blackberries, and black currants.

Red Berry Sherbet

INGREDIENTS
1¼ cups red currants, plus extra
    to decorate
1¼ cups raspberries, plus extra
    to decorate
¾ cup water
generous ½ cup sugar
⅔ cup cranberry juice
2 egg whites

CAUTION
*Recipes using raw eggs should be
avoided by infants, the elderly, pregnant
women, convalescents, and anyone
suffering from an illness.*

SERVES 6
Strip the red currants from their stalks using the tines of a fork and put them in a large heavy-bottom pan together with the raspberries. Add 2 tablespoons of the water and cook over medium heat for 10 minutes, or until soft. Push the fruit through a nylon strainer into a bowl to form a purée.

Put the sugar and the remaining water into the rinsed-out pan and heat gently, stirring, until the sugar has dissolved. Bring to a boil, then boil, without stirring, for 10 minutes to form a syrup. Do not let it brown. Remove from the heat and let cool for at least 1 hour. When cold, stir the fruit purée and cranberry juice into the syrup.

If using an ice-cream machine, churn the mixture in the machine following the manufacturer's instructions. When the mixture starts to freeze, whisk the egg whites until they just hold their shape but are not dry, then add to the mixture and continue churning. Alternatively, freeze the mixture in a freezerproof container, uncovered, for 3–4 hours, or until mushy. Turn the mixture into a bowl and stir with a fork or beat in a food processor to break down the ice crystals. Lightly whisk the egg whites until stiff but not dry, then fold them into the mixture. Return to the freezer and freeze for an additional 3–4 hours, or until firm or required. Cover the container with a lid for storing. Serve sprinkled with extra fruits.

The recipe suggests pushing the kiwifruit purée through a strainer to remove the seeds, but, if you prefer, you can omit this so that the sherbet is flecked with the dark seeds.

Kiwifruit Sherbet

SERVES 6

Put the sugar and water in a heavy-bottom pan and heat gently, stirring, until the sugar has dissolved. Bring to a boil, then let simmer, without stirring, for 2 minutes. Remove from the heat and let cool for at least 1 hour.

Using a sharp knife, thinly peel the kiwifruit. Put the flesh in a food processor or blender, add the syrup, and process to form a smooth purée. Push the purée through a nylon strainer into a bowl to remove the seeds, if preferred.

If using an ice-cream machine, churn the mixture in the machine following the manufacturer's instructions. When the mixture starts to freeze, whisk the egg whites until they just hold their shape but are not dry, then add to the mixture and continue churning. Alternatively, freeze the mixture in a freezerproof container, uncovered, for 3 hours, or until mushy. Turn the mixture into a bowl and stir with a fork or beat in a food processor to break down the ice crystals. Lightly whisk the egg whites until stiff but not dry, then fold them into the mixture. Return the sherbet to the freezer and freeze for an additional 3–4 hours, or until firm or required. Cover the container with a lid for storing. Serve decorated with the extra kiwifruit, peeled and sliced.

INGREDIENTS
generous ¼ cup sugar
⅔ cup water
8 kiwifruit, plus 2 extra to decorate
2 egg whites

CAUTION
Recipes using raw eggs should be avoided by infants, the elderly, pregnant women, convalescents, and anyone suffering from an illness.

The lemon rind and juice added to the basic sugar syrup complement the delicate flavor of the passion fruit extremely well. The addition of gelatin helps to produce a smooth texture.

Passion Fruit Sherbet

INGREDIENTS
1½ cups water
1 tsp granulated gelatin
generous 1¼ cups sugar
grated rind and juice of 2 lemons
8 passion fruit, plus 2 extra, to serve

SERVES 6
Put 2 tablespoons of the water in a small bowl and sprinkle in the gelatin. Let soak for 5 minutes.

Meanwhile, put the remaining water, the sugar, and lemon rind in a heavy-bottom pan and heat gently, stirring, until the sugar has dissolved. Bring to a boil, then let simmer, without stirring, for 2 minutes. Remove from the heat.

Add the soaked gelatin to the syrup and stir until dissolved. Stir in the lemon juice. Cut the passion fruit in half and, holding them over the syrup, scoop out the seeds with a teaspoon into the syrup. Let the syrup cool, then let chill in the refrigerator for 2 hours, or until cold. When cold, strain the syrup through a nylon strainer into a bowl.

If using an ice-cream machine, churn the mixture in the machine following the manufacturer's instructions. Alternatively, freeze the mixture in a freezerproof container, uncovered, for 3–4 hours, or until mushy. Turn the mixture into a bowl and stir with a fork or beat in a food processor to break down the ice crystals. Return to the freezer and freeze for an additional 3–4 hours, or until firm or required. Cover the container with a lid for storing. Serve decorated with the scooped-out seeds of the extra passion fruit spooned over the top.

If you would prefer the sherbet to contain lemon rind, finely grate the rind and add it to the sugar syrup—there is no need to strain it.

Lemon Water Ice

SERVES 6

Put the sugar and water in a heavy-bottom pan and heat gently, stirring, until the sugar has dissolved. Bring to a boil, then boil, without stirring, for 10 minutes to form a syrup. Do not let it brown.

Meanwhile, using a potato peeler, thinly pare the rind from 4 of the lemons. Remove the syrup from the heat and add the pared lemon rind. Let cool for at least 1 hour.

Squeeze the juice from the lemons and strain into a measuring cup—you need scant 2 cups in total. When the syrup is cold, strain it into a bowl, add the lemon juice, and stir together until well mixed.

If using an ice-cream machine, churn the mixture in the machine following the manufacturer's instructions. Alternatively, freeze the mixture in a freezerproof container, uncovered, for 3–4 hours, or until mushy. Turn the mixture into a bowl and stir with a fork or beat in a food processor to break down the ice crystals. Return to the freezer and freeze for an additional 3–4 hours, or until firm or required. Cover the container with a lid for storing. Serve decorated with lemon slices.

INGREDIENTS
scant 1 cup sugar
scant 2 cups water
6–9 large lemons
lemon slices, to decorate

Gooseberries and elderberry flowers are perfect partners. Elderberry flower cordial has been used in this recipe as it is more readily available than freshly picked elderberry flower heads.

Gooseberry & Elderberry Flower Sherbet

INGREDIENTS
generous ½ cup sugar
2½ cups water
1 lb 2 oz/500 g fresh gooseberries
½ cup elderberry flower cordial
1 tbsp lemon juice
few drops of green food coloring
    (optional)
½ cup heavy cream

SERVES 6

Put the sugar and water in a large heavy-bottom pan and heat gently, stirring, until the sugar has dissolved. Bring to a boil, then add the gooseberries, without trimming them, and let simmer, stirring occasionally, for 10 minutes, or until very tender. Let cool for 5 minutes.

Put the gooseberries in a food processor or blender and process to form a smooth purée. Push the purée through a nylon strainer into a bowl to remove the seeds. Let cool for at least 1 hour.

Add the elderberry flower cordial and lemon juice to the cold gooseberry purée and stir together until well mixed. If wished, add the food coloring to tint the mixture pale green. Stir the cream into the mixture.

If using an ice-cream machine, churn the mixture in the machine following the manufacturer's instructions. Alternatively, freeze the mixture in a freezerproof container, uncovered, for 3–4 hours, or until mushy. Turn the mixture into a bowl and stir with a fork or beat in a food processor to break down the ice crystals. Return to the freezer and freeze for an additional 3–4 hours, or until firm or required. Cover the container with a lid for storing.

A parfait is a rich, creamy ice. It is made from a sugar syrup, which is poured over whisked egg whites and whisked until it is thick, creamy and voluminous. It is often flavored with a liqueur.

Raspberry Parfait

SERVES 6

Put the raspberries in a food processor or blender and process to form a smooth purée. Push through a nylon strainer into a bowl to remove the seeds. Sift the confectioners' sugar into the raspberry purée, then stir together until well mixed. Stir in the Kirsch or cherry brandy, if using.

Put the granulated sugar and water in a small heavy-bottom pan and heat gently, stirring, until the sugar has dissolved. Bring to a boil, then boil, without stirring, for 5 minutes, or until a syrup has formed. Do not let it brown. Meanwhile, whisk the egg whites until stiff and dry

Drizzle the hot syrup in a thin stream onto the whisked egg whites, whisking all the time until the mixture is thick, creamy and fluffy. Continue whisking until the mixture is cold.

Whip the cream until stiff. Fold the raspberry purée into the egg white mixture, then fold in the whipped cream.

Freeze the raspberry mixture in a freezerproof container, uncovered, for 3–4 hours, or until firm or required. Cover the container with a lid for storing. Serve sprinkled with raspberries.

INGREDIENTS

1 lb/450 g fresh raspberries, plus extra to decorate
¾ cup confectioners' sugar
1 tbsp Kirsch or cherry brandy (optional)
scant ½ cup granulated sugar
½ cup water
2 egg whites
1¼ cups heavy whipping cream

CAUTION

Recipes using raw eggs should be avoided by infants, the elderly, pregnant women, convalescents, and anyone suffering from an illness.

This is a particularly refreshing sherbet to serve on a hot summer's day or as a dessert to follow a substantial meal. Other suitable teas are Earl Grey and peppermint.

Green Tea Sherbet

INGREDIENTS
3½ cups water
scant 1 cup sugar
4 tbsp Japanese green tea leaves
2 tbsp lemon juice
2 egg whites

CAUTION
Recipes using raw eggs should be avoided by infants, the elderly, pregnant women, convalescents, and anyone suffering from an illness.

SERVES 6
Put 2½ cups of the water in a heavy-bottom pan, add the sugar and heat gently, stirring, until the sugar has dissolved. Bring to a boil, then let simmer, without stirring, for 10 minutes to form a syrup. Do not let it brown. Remove from the heat and let cool for at least 1 hour.

Meanwhile, bring the remaining water to a boil. Pour over the tea leaves and let infuse for 10 minutes. Strain the tea liquid. When the syrup is cold, add the strained tea and lemon juice and stir together until well mixed.

If using an ice-cream machine, churn the mixture in the machine following the manufacturer's instructions. When the mixture starts to freeze, whisk the egg whites until they just hold their shape but are not dry, then fold into the mixture and continue churning. Alternatively, freeze the mixture in a freezerproof container, uncovered, for 3–4 hours, or until mushy. Turn the mixture into a bowl and stir with a fork or beat in a food processor to break down the ice crystals. Lightly whisk the egg whites until they just hold their shape but are not dry, then fold them into the mixture. Return to the freezer and freeze for an additional 3–4 hours, until firm or required. Cover the container with a lid for storing.

frozen

frozen assets

The recipes in this chapter are, as the title suggests, useful, valuable assets. The joy is that they can be made in advance and stored in the freezer. There they can be kept and brought out just before serving for a special occasion. Christmas Pudding Ice Cream falls into this category, as does Sicilian Bombe. Then there is Zabaglione Semifreddo, an impressive ice cream version of the classic Italian dessert.

These are sophisticated frozen desserts. Layered, studded with fruit and nuts, packed with contrasting flavors, colors, and textures, they are perfect for entertaining. You will find elegant bombes and terrines, many of which appear elaborate but are no more complicated or time-consuming to make than the other ice cream recipes in this book. Most are based on a rich egg custard, which, although it needs watching, is not difficult to make. No specific molds are needed—ordinary ovenproof bowls and rectangular plastic boxes will suffice.

Don't start to panic when you come to the unmolding stage! This can either be done as soon as you take the ice cream out of the freezer by quickly dipping the mold into hot water, or you can leave the ice cream at room temperature, then slide it out of its mold. If ice creams look a bit fuzzy around the edges, pop them back into the freezer for 5 minutes to firm up again. Turned out onto serving dishes, these are the crowning glory of ice creams. Take advantage of them.

This Sicilian ice cream is also known as cassata Gelato but should not be confused with cassata Siciliana, the classic frozen dessert made with ricotta cheese and sponge cake.

Sicilian Bombe

INGREDIENTS

2½ cups whole milk
5 egg yolks
generous ½ cup superfine sugar
finely grated rind of 1 lemon
⅔ cup heavy whipping cream
1 tbsp confectioners' sugar
2 tbsp chopped candied peel
2 tbsp candied cherries, chopped
1 tbsp shelled pistachios, chopped

SERVES 6–8

Put a 5-cup ovenproof bowl in the freezer. Pour the milk into a heavy-bottom pan and bring almost to a boil. Remove from the heat. Put the egg yolks and superfine sugar in a large bowl and whisk together until pale and the mixture leaves a trail when the whisk is lifted. Slowly add the milk, stirring all the time with a wooden spoon.

Strain the mixture into the rinsed-out pan or a double boiler and cook over low heat for 10–15 minutes, stirring all the time, until the mixture thickens enough to coat the back of the spoon. Do not let the mixture boil or it will curdle.

Remove the custard from the heat, stir in the lemon rind, then let cool for at least 1 hour, stirring from time to time to prevent a skin forming. If using an ice-cream machine, churn the cold custard in the machine following the manufacturer's instructions. Alternatively, freeze the custard in a freezerproof container, uncovered, for 1–2 hours, or until it starts to set around the edges. Turn the custard into a bowl and stir with a fork or beat in a food processor until smooth. Return to the freezer and freeze for an additional 2–3 hours, or until firm. Remove from the freezer and beat again until smooth. Spoon the frozen ice cream into the chilled ovenproof bowl and, using the spoon, line the bottom and sides with it, leaving a hole in the center. Freeze for 1 hour, or until firm.

Whip the cream until it holds its shape. Sift the confectioners' sugar into the cream, add the candied peel, cherries, and nuts, and fold in. Spoon the mixture into the center of the frozen ice cream. Cover the bowl and return to

the freezer for an additional 4 hours, or until firm or required. Take the ice cream out of the freezer about 30 minutes before you are ready to serve it. Uncover, place a serving plate over the bowl, invert it, and leave at room temperature. If it is not possible to remove the bowl by the time you wish to serve it, stand it in hot water for a few seconds to loosen it, then lift it off.

This ice cream, rich in fruit and nuts, is perfect to serve as an alternative to the traditional Christmas pudding.

Christmas Pudding Ice Cream

INGREDIENTS
generous ¼ cup candied cherries
generous ¼ cup no-soak dried apricots
1 cup mixed dried fruit
5 tbsp sherry
scant 2 cups whole milk
3 eggs
generous ½ cup superfine sugar
1¼ cups heavy cream
⅔ cup light cream
2 tbsp chopped blanched almonds
1 holly sprig, to decorate

SERVES 8

Halve the cherries and cut the apricots into small pieces about the same size. Put in a bowl, add the mixed dried fruit and sherry, and stir together. Let soak for 2–3 hours, stirring occasionally, until the sherry is absorbed.

Meanwhile, pour the milk into a heavy-bottom pan and bring almost to a boil. Remove from the heat. Put the eggs and sugar in a large bowl and whisk together until pale and the mixture leaves a trail when the whisk is lifted. Slowly add the milk, stirring all the time with a wooden spoon. Strain the mixture into the rinsed-out pan or a double boiler and cook over low heat for 10–15 minutes, stirring all the time, until the mixture thickens enough to coat the back of the spoon. Do not let the mixture boil or it will curdle. Remove the custard from the heat and let cool for at least 1 hour, stirring from time to time to prevent a skin forming.

Meanwhile, whip the heavy cream and light cream together until the mixture holds its shape. Keep in the refrigerator until ready to use.

If using an ice-cream machine, fold the cold custard into the whipped cream, then churn it in the machine following the manufacturer's instructions. Just before the ice cream freezes, turn it into a large bowl and stir in the soaked fruits and nuts. Alternatively, freeze the custard in a freezerproof container, uncovered, for 1–2 hours, or until it starts to set around the edges. Turn the custard into a bowl and stir with a fork or beat in a food processor until smooth. Fold in the whipped cream, soaked fruits, and nuts. Pack the ice

cream into a 7¼-cup ovenproof bowl, cover and freeze for an additional 3–4 hours, or until firm or required.

Take the ice cream out of the freezer about 30 minutes before you are ready to serve it. Uncover, place a serving plate over the bowl, invert it, and leave at room temperature. If it is not possible to remove the bowl by the time you wish to serve it, stand it in hot water for a few seconds to loosen it, then lift it off. Serve decorated with a sprig of holly.

This is an Italian ice cream, but "semifreddo" means that it is softer than the traditional gelato. It is made with egg whites, which are whisked until they are stiff. Hot sugar syrup is then added.

Cassata Semifreddo

SERVES 6–8

Line a 2-lb/900-g loaf pan or 6-cup oblong freezerproof plastic container with waxed paper, allowing it to hang over the edges of the container so that the ice cream can be easily removed. Put the sugar and water in a small heavy-bottom pan and heat gently, stirring, until the sugar has dissolved. Bring to a boil, then boil, without stirring, for 5 minutes, or until a syrup has formed. Do not let it brown.

Meanwhile, whisk the egg whites until stiff and dry. Drizzle the hot syrup in a thin stream onto the whisked egg whites, whisking all the time until the mixture is thick, creamy and fluffy. Continue whisking until the mixture is cold.

Add the nuts, dried fruit, and cherries to the meringue mixture and fold in until well blended. Whip the cream until it holds its shape, then fold in until well blended. Pour the mixture into the prepared pan or plastic container, cover, and freeze for 5 hours, or until firm or required.

To serve the ice cream, uncover, stand the pan or plastic container in hot water for a few seconds to loosen it, then invert it onto a serving dish. Remove the waxed paper and, using a hot knife, cut into slices.

INGREDIENTS

generous ½ cup granulated sugar
⅔ cup water
2 egg whites
scant ⅓ cup chopped blanched almonds
scant ⅓ cup mixed dried fruit
scant ⅓ cup candied cherries, chopped
1¼ cups heavy whipping cream

CAUTION
Recipes using raw eggs should be avoided by infants, the elderly, pregnant women, convalescents, and anyone suffering from an illness.

Zabaglione, the well-known Italian egg custard and Marsala dessert, is usually served immediately it is cooked but, as this recipe proves, it is also delicious served as an ice cream!

Zabaglione Semifreddo

INGREDIENTS
4 egg yolks
½ cup superfine sugar
generous ⅓ cup dry Marsala
scant 1 cup heavy whipping cream
shortbread cookies, to serve

SERVES 4–6

Put the egg yolks and sugar in a large heatproof bowl and whisk together until pale and the mixture leaves a trail when the whisk is lifted. Whisk in the Marsala, a tablespoon at a time, until well blended.

Place the bowl over a pan of simmering water and heat gently, whisking all the time, until the mixture has doubled in quantity. Remove the bowl from the heat, stand the bowl in cold water, and whisk until the mixture is cool.

Whip the cream until it holds its shape. Add the whipped cream to the egg mixture, then fold in until well blended.

Freeze the mixture in a freezerproof container, uncovered, for 2–3 hours, or until firm or required. Cover the container with a lid for storing.

Serve in small, tall glasses, accompanied by cookies.

This popular Italian ice cream was created by a Mr Tortoni, who opened the first Neapolitan café in Paris in the nineteenth century, and it was here that it became famous.

Cookie Tortoni

SERVES 6

Line a 1-lb/450-g loaf pan or 3½-cup oblong freezerproof plastic container with waxed paper, allowing it to hang over the edges of the container so that the ice cream can be easily removed. Put the cookies in a food processor and process to form fine crumbs. Alternatively, put the cookies in a strong plastic bag and crush with a rolling pin.

Pour the heavy cream and light cream into a large bowl and whip together until the mixture holds its shape. Sift the confectioners' sugar into the whipped cream, then fold in with the Marsala. Fold in the cookies, reserving a third.

Pour the mixture into the prepared pan or plastic container, smooth the surface and freeze, uncovered, for 5 hours, or until firm or required. Cover the container with a lid for storing.

Take the ice cream out of the freezer about 30 minutes before you are ready to serve it. Uncover, turn out onto a serving dish, and remove the waxed paper. Leave at room temperature to soften. Using a palette knife, press the reserved crushed cookies lightly onto the top and sides of the ice cream until it is evenly coated. Serve cut into thick slices.

INGREDIENTS

4½ oz/125 g amaretti cookies
1¼ cups heavy cream
⅔ cup light cream
1 cup confectioners' sugar
4 tbsp Marsala

Deliciously fresh-tasting, the tangy lemon and orange flavors of this ice cream combine brilliantly with the sweet caramel sauce.

Iced Citrus Terrine with Caramel Sauce

INGREDIENTS
4 egg yolks
2 tbsp superfine sugar
1¼ cups heavy whipping cream
finely grated rind and juice of 1 orange
finely grated rind of 1 lemon
3 oranges, segmented, to serve
CARAMEL SAUCE
scant ⅔ cup sugar
½ cup water
1 tbsp lemon juice
⅔ cup light cream

CAUTION
Recipes using raw eggs should be avoided by infants, the elderly, pregnant women, convalescents, and anyone suffering from an illness.

SERVES 6
Line a 1 lb 9-oz/700-g loaf pan or 5-cup oblong freezerproof plastic container with waxed paper, allowing it to hang over the edges of the container so that the ice cream can be easily removed. To make the citrus terrine, put the egg yolks and sugar in a large bowl and whisk together until pale and the mixture leaves a trail when the whisk is lifted.

Whip the cream until it holds its shape. Fold into the egg mixture, then fold in the grated orange and lemon rind and the orange juice. Do not worry if the mixture appears too runny at this stage.

Pour the mixture into the prepared pan or plastic container, cover and freeze for 4 hours, or until firm or required.

To make the caramel sauce, put the sugar, water, and lemon juice in a heavy-bottom pan and heat gently, stirring, until the sugar has dissolved. Bring to a boil, then cook, without stirring, for 5 minutes, or until the mixture turns to a pale caramel color. Remove from the heat and stir in the cream. Let the sauce cool, then let chill in the refrigerator for at least 3 hours.

To serve the ice cream, uncover, stand the pan or plastic container in hot water for a few seconds to loosen it, then invert it onto a serving dish. Remove the waxed paper and, using a hot knife, cut the terrine into slices. Serve with the orange segments and accompany with the caramel sauce.

A dessert to make in the summer when raspberries are plentiful and tuck away in the freezer, to be eaten any time of year!

Raspberry Macaroon Bombe

SERVES 6

Put the cookies in a food processor and process to form coarse crumbs. Alternatively, put the cookies in a strong plastic bag and crush with a rolling pin. Put the crumbs in a bowl, add the Kirsch, and let soak for 30 minutes.

Meanwhile, put the raspberries in a food processor or blender and process to form a purée. Add the superfine sugar and mix well together. Pour the raspberry mixture into a bowl.

Pour the heavy cream and light cream into a large bowl and whip together until the mixture holds its shape. Add a third of the whipped cream to the cookie mixture and fold in until well blended. Add another third of the cream to the raspberry mixture and fold in. Sift the unsweetened cocoa and confectioners' sugar over the remaining third of the cream, then fold into the cream until thoroughly incorporated.

Put the macaroon mixture in the bottom of a 6-cup ovenproof bowl. Add the chocolate cream and spread over to form a layer, then add the raspberry mixture. Cover the bowl and freeze for 5 hours, or until firm or required.

Take the ice cream out of the freezer about 30 minutes before you are ready to serve it. Uncover, place a serving plate over the bowl, invert it, and leave at room temperature. If it is not possible to remove the bowl by the time you wish to serve it, stand in hot water for a few seconds to loosen it, then lift it off.

INGREDIENTS
4½ oz/125 g amaretti cookies
2 tbsp Kirsch or cherry brandy
generous 1½ cups fresh raspberries
¼ cup superfine sugar
1¼ cups heavy cream
⅔ cup light cream
3 tbsp unsweetened cocoa
2 tbsp confectioners' sugar

The red currant sprigs suggested for decorating can be frozen so that you have them when you are ready to serve the ice cream. Freeze the whole sprigs and they keep their shape.

Iced Red Currant & Mascarpone Terrine

INGREDIENTS

1¼ cups fresh red currants, plus
    extra sprigs to decorate
finely grated rind and juice of
    1 large orange
2 tbsp confectioners' sugar
generous 1 cup mascarpone cheese
⅔ cup heavy whipping cream

SERVES 6

Line a 1-lb/450-g loaf pan or 3½-cup oblong freezerproof plastic container with waxed paper, allowing it to hang over the edges of the container so that the ice cream can be easily removed. Strip the red currants from their stalks using the tines of a fork and put in a bowl. Using the back of a wooden spoon, crush the red currants.

Add the orange rind and juice to the red currants and mix together. Sift in the confectioners' sugar, then mix well. Add the mascarpone and mix until well blended. Whip the cream until it holds its shape. Add to the red currant mixture and fold in until well blended.

Turn the mixture into the prepared pan or plastic container, smooth the surface and freeze, uncovered, for 4 hours, or until firm or required. Cover the container with a lid for storing.

To serve the ice cream, uncover, stand the pan or plastic container in hot water for a few seconds to loosen it, then invert it onto a serving dish. Remove the waxed paper and, using a hot knife, cut the terrine into slices. Serve decorated with red currant sprigs.

Nesselrode is the name given to a selection of dishes, all of which contain chestnut purée. It is named after a nineteenth-century Russian diplomat, and is an ideal dessert to serve at Christmas.

Nesselrode Bombe

INGREDIENTS
1 cup mixed dried fruit
4 tbsp Kirsch or cherry brandy
1¼ cups light cream
1 vanilla bean
4 egg yolks
scant ½ cup superfine sugar
9 oz/250 g canned peeled chestnuts
1¼ cups heavy cream
generous ¼ cup candied cherries, chopped

SERVES 8

Put the dried fruit in a bowl, add the Kirsch and stir together. Let soak for 2–3 hours, stirring occasionally, until the liquid is absorbed. Meanwhile, pour the light cream into a heavy-bottom pan, add the vanilla bean, and bring almost to a boil. Remove from the heat and let infuse for 15 minutes.

Put the egg yolks and sugar in a large bowl and whisk together until pale and the mixture leaves a trail when the whisk is lifted. Remove the vanilla bean from the cream, then slowly add the cream to the egg mixture, stirring all the time with a wooden spoon.

Strain the mixture into the rinsed-out pan or a double boiler and cook over low heat for 10–15 minutes, stirring all the time, until the mixture thickens enough to coat the back of the spoon. Do not let the mixture boil or it will curdle. Remove the custard from the heat and let cool for at least 1 hour, stirring from time to time to prevent a skin forming.

Put the chestnuts in a food processor or blender and process to form a purée. Whip the heavy cream until it just holds its shape. Fold in the soaked fruits and the cherries until well blended.

When the custard is cold, add the chestnut purée and whisk together. Fold in the cream and fruit mixture, then pour into a 6-cup ovenproof bowl, cover, and freeze for 5 hours, or until firm or required.

Take the ice cream out of the freezer about 30 minutes before you are ready to serve it. Uncover, place a serving plate over the bowl, invert it, and leave at room temperature. If it is not possible to remove the bowl by the time you wish to serve it, stand it in hot water for a few seconds to loosen it, then lift it off.

Chocolate and ice cream have to be one of the most delicious dessert combinations of all. This makes an ideal dinner-party dessert as it can be prepared ahead.

Chocolate Peppermint Crisp Terrine

INGREDIENTS

1¼ cups light cream
½ tsp peppermint extract
4 egg yolks
½ cup superfine sugar
7 oz/200 g semisweet chocolate peppermint crisps
1¼ cups heavy cream
chocolate leaves, to decorate

SERVES 6–8

Line a 1-lb/450-g loaf pan or 3½-cup oblong freezerproof plastic container with waxed paper, allowing it to hang over the edges of the container so that the ice cream can be easily removed. Pour the light cream into a heavy-bottom pan and bring almost to a boil. Remove from the heat and stir in the peppermint extract.

Put the egg yolks and sugar in a large bowl and whisk together until pale and the mixture leaves a trail when the whisk is lifted. Slowly add the cream, stirring all the time with a wooden spoon.

Strain the mixture into the rinsed-out pan or a double boiler and cook over low heat for 10–15 minutes, stirring all the time, until the mixture thickens enough to coat the back of the spoon. Do not let the mixture boil or it will curdle. Remove the custard from the heat and let cool for at least 1 hour, stirring from time to time to prevent a skin forming.

Meanwhile, put the peppermint crisps, a few at a time, into a food processor and chop into small pieces. Alternatively, chop the peppermint crisps into small pieces by hand.

Whip the heavy cream until it just holds its shape. When the custard is cold, stir in the peppermint crisp pieces, then fold in the whipped cream until well blended.

Turn the mixture into the prepared pan or plastic container and then freeze, uncovered, for 4 hours, or until firm or required. Cover the container with a lid for storing.

To serve the ice cream, uncover, stand the pan or plastic container in hot water for a few seconds to loosen it, then invert it onto a serving dish. Remove the waxed paper and, using a hot knife, cut the terrine into slices. Serve decorated with the chocolate leaves.

index